Looking
for the
Queen

by Gordon L. Storey
illustrated by
Steven Wolfgang

Scott Foresman

Editorial Offices: Glenview, Illinois • New York, New York
Sales Offices: Reading, Massachusetts • Duluth, Georgia
Glenview, Illinois • Carrollton, Texas • Menlo Park, California

Calls, calls, calls!

There are calls for the queen.

Do you know where she is?

Letters, letters, letters!
There are letters for the queen.
Do you know where she is?

But the queen was having fun.

She was happy.